THE
IMPERFECT
Sand
DOLLAR

ISBN: 978-0-692-08642-1

10 9 8 7 6 5 4 3 2 1

Editor: Lucy Herring Chambers
Designer: Marla Y. Garcia

Printed in Canada through Friesens

THE
IMPERFECT
Sand
DOLLAR

MARGARET WALLACE ROTAN

For Doug, Patricia,
Mary Margaret & Douglas

"So God created man in his own image,
in the image of God he created him;
male and female he created them."

GENESIS 1:27

"For we are God's workmanship, created in
Christ Jesus to do good works, which God
prepared in advance for us to do."

EPHESIANS 2:10

EVERY *human* IS CREATED
IN THE IMAGE OF GOD.

LIKE A *perfect* SAND DOLLAR
WE FIND ON THE BEACH.

"The Lord himself goes before you and will
be with you; he will never leave you
nor forsake you. Do not be afraid;
do not be discouraged."

DEUTERONOMY 31:8

"Blessed are those who mourn,
for they will be comforted."

MATTHEW 5:4

THROUGHOUT *our* LIFE,
WE EXPERIENCE

SADNESS, LONELINESS
AND *fear*.

"The Lord is close to the brokenhearted
and saves those who are
crushed in spirit."

PSALM 34:18

• • ● • • • •

"He will wipe every tear from their eyes.
There will be no more death or mourning
or crying or pain, for the old order
of things has passed away."

REVELATION 21:4

WE EXPERIENCE PAIN

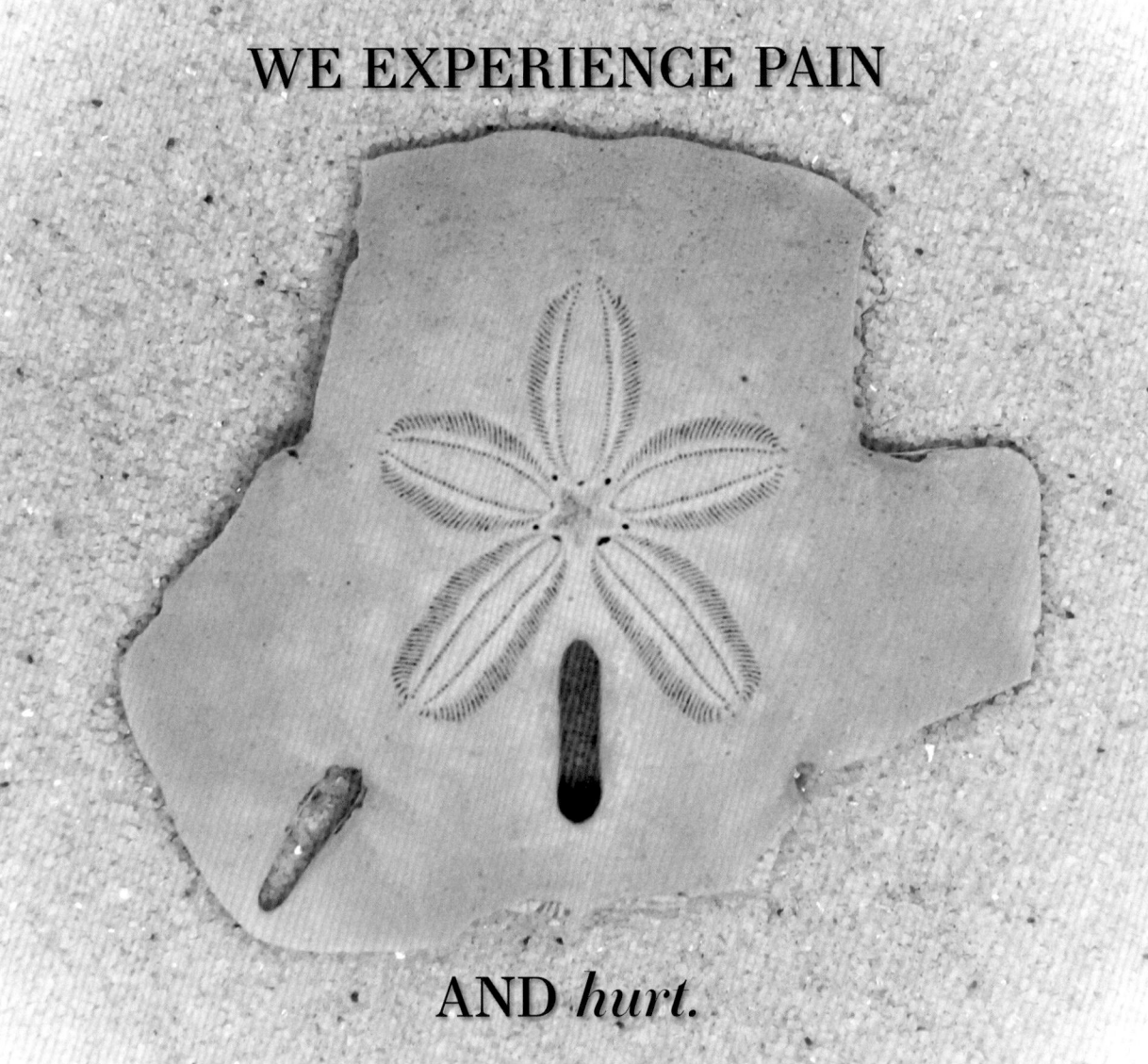

AND *hurt.*

"If the Lord delights in a man's way, he makes
his steps firm; though he may stumble,
he will not fall, for the Lord upholds
him with his hand."

PSALM 37:23-24

· · ● · ● · ·

"If we confess our sins, he is faithful and just
and will forgive us our sins and purify us
from all unrighteousness."

1 JOHN 1:9

AS *humans*
WE MAKE MISTAKES

AND *wrong* TURNS.

"Trust in the Lord with all your heart and
lean not on your own understanding;
in all ways, acknowledge him,
and he will make your paths straight."

PROVERBS 3:5-6

"Your kingdom is an everlasting kingdom, and your
dominion endures through all generations.
The Lord is faithful to all his promises
and loving toward all he has made."

PSALM 145:13

BUT WITHIN US ALWAYS ARE
God's PROMISES.

FAITH, HOPE, GRACE,
PEACE, AND *Love*

"I have chosen my way of faithfulness;
I have set my heart on your laws."

PSALM 119:30

• • ● • • •

"We live by faith, not by sight."

2 CORINTHIANS 5:7

• • ● • • •

"Be strong and take heart, all you who
hope in the Lord."

PSALM 31:24

• • ● • • •

"For I know the plans I have for you," declares the LORD,
"plans to prosper you and not to harm you,
plans to give you hope and a future."

JEREMIAH 29:11

"You are the most excellent of men and your lips
have been annointed with grace, since God
has blessed you forever."

PSALM 45:2

• • ● • ● •

"From the fullness of his grace we have all received
one blessing after another."

JOHN 1:16

• • ● • ● •

"You will keep in perfect peace him whose mind
is steadfast, because he trusts in you."

ISAIAH 26:3

• • ● • ● •

"These things I have spoken to you, that in Me
you may have peace. In the world you
will have tribulation; but be of good
cheer, I have overcome the world"

JOHN 16:33

"But you, O Lord, are a compassionate and
gracious God, slow to anger, abounding
in love and faithfulness."

PSALM 86:15

• ◦ ● • ● • •

"How great is the love the Father has lavished on us,
that we should be called children of God!"

1 JOHN 3:1

• ◦ ● • ● • •

"And now these three remain: faith, hope and love.
But the greatest of these is love."

1 CORINTHIANS 13:13

• ◦ ● • ● • •

"Do everything in love."

1 CORINTHIANS 16:14

NO MATTER WHAT WE
go through IN LIFE,

God's promises ARE ALWAYS
WITH US.

THE LEGEND OF THE
SAND DOLLAR

There's a pretty little legend
That I would like to tell
Of the birth and the death of Jesus
Found in this lowly shell.

If you examine closely,
You'll see that you find here
Four nail holes and a fifth one
Made by a Roman's spear.

On one side the Easter lily,
It's center is the star
That appeared unto the shepherds
And led them from afar.

The Christmas poinsettia
Etched on the other side
Reminds us of His birthday,
Our happy Christmastide.

Now break the center open
And here you will release
The five doves awaiting
To spread Good Will and Peace

This simple little symbol,
Christ left for you and me
To help us spread His Gospel
Through all eternity.

— Author Unknown —

ABOUT THE AUTHOR

• • • • • •

MARGARET WALLACE ROTAN, a fourth generation Houstonian, is a professional photographer. She and her husband, Doug, have three grown children. She and her family have spent countless summers along the Gulf Coast in Port O'Connor, Texas, combing the beach for sand dollars, which have served as a spiritual touchstone for her throughout her life. When Hurricane Harvey hit Houston in August 2017, Margaret and her family lost their home to the extensive flooding. In the aftermath of the storm, Margaret found herself relying on her faith more than ever, and this experience encouraged her to create *The Imperfect Sand Dollar*.